rimertown

an atlas

NEW CALIFORNIA POETRY

Edited by Robert Hass, Calvin Bedient,
Brenda Hillman, and Forrest Gander

For, by Carol Snow
Enola Gay, by Mark Levine
Selected Poems, by Fanny Howe
Sleeping with the Dictionary, by Harryette Mullen
Commons, by Myung Mi Kim
The Guns and Flags Project, by Geoffrey G. O'Brien
Gone, by Fanny Howe
Why / Why Not, by Martha Ronk
A Carnage in the Lovetrees, by Richard Greenfield
The Seventy Prepositions, by Carol Snow
Not Even Then, by Brian Blanchfield
Facts for Visitors, by Srikanth Reddy
Weather Eye Open, by Sarah Gridley
Subject, by Laura Mullen
This Connection of Everyone with Lungs, by Juliana Spahr
The Totality for Kids, by Joshua Clover
The Wilds, by Mark Levine
I Love Artists, by Mei-mei Berssenbrugge
Harm., by Steve Willard
Green and Gray, by Geoffrey G. O'Brien
The Age of Huts (compleat), by Ron Silliman
It's go in horizontal: Selected Poems, 1974–2006, by Leslie Scalapino
rimertown / an atlas, by Laura Walker
Ours, by Cole Swensen

rimertown

an atlas

poems

Laura Walker

UNIVERSITY OF CALIFORNIA PRESS

BERKELEY   LOS ANGELES   LONDON

This project is supported in part by an award from the National
Endowment for the Arts.

NATIONAL
ENDOWMENT
FOR THE ARTS
A great nation
deserves great art.

University of California Press, one of the most distinguished
university presses in the United States, enriches lives around the
world by advancing scholarship in the humanities, social sciences,
and natural sciences. Its activities are supported by the UC Press
Foundation and by philanthropic contributions from individuals
and institutions. For more information, visit www.ucpress.edu.

University of California Press
Berkeley and Los Angeles, California

University of California Press, Ltd.
London, England

Library of Congress Cataloging-in-Publication Data

Walker, Laura, 1966–.
  rimertown / an atlas / Laura Walker.
    p.   cm. — (New California poetry ; 23)
  ISBN 978-0-520-25459-6 (cloth : alk. paper)
  ISBN 978-0-520-25460-2 (pbk : alk. paper)
  I. Title.
  PS3623.A35949R56 2008
  811'.6—dc22   2007033569

Manufactured in Canada

17 16 15 14 13 12 11 10 09 08
10 9 8 7 6 5 4 3 2 1

The paper used in this publication meets the minimum require-
ments of ANSI/NISO z39.48-1992 (R1997) (*Permanence of Paper*).

for daddy lou and mama ruth

who brought us there

acknowledgments

Much gratitude to the editors of *Sentence* and *Big Ugly Review* who first published some of these poems.

A thousand thanks to Valerie Coulton, Ed Smallfield, Stephen Hemenway, and Laynie Browne for their invaluable comments on the manuscript, and to the many others who responded to individual poems.

And countless thanks, always, to my family.

canticle for rimertown

as if a pond
as if a letter

gravelly
interstices, a judgment
that all will be

butternut squash, poor chickens

lint and return
i am lidded i am wake

girl on a rockinghorse

(tuesdays were for pulling)
location. primacy of place

(bless your heart)
water kept (where all night)
flowing

and scattered seed with a single throw
(her pillow) scattered there

as if a cant
as if a leaden soldier

discovered all at once
later in the sawdust

rimertown

an atlas

map 42

cast
against shape and shore
(she) meanders slowly
a little leg
letting in the light

(praise her   praise

that in falling off the edge
sinewy and stiff, lines merging
we come back to idea
parchment

and that once was. huddled by a church not built. we are, in its shadows
and with another turn a spire. rises deep shadow and the graveyard. will
be the marker

birds falling out of their nests

asphalt opening up, heat against our heels

at the top of the hill, and below. the line between lake and pond, and private
anyway: there at the end of the foxes' road. that down we would swoop

we stood and caught them as they fell

3

mountain ash carried starkly through woods. left out on the porch overnight. arms torn in cinders, they were mountain people. it couldn't have stood all night, that's memory playing. fog playing. they carried him backwards to fool the devil, lowered him just as they said they were. someone singing the other side of the church. shedevil. come a little closer and croon that one to me

map 17

cull   call

a cardinal in the yard. bent to rights over water
to learn the song of a mockingbird, brittle white
litmus over time
bring lime from water
shallow, welt streams

told not to dive
a foot a sleep
bachelor buttons lining the field
we knew him to come running.   thirst, the oven left on
we knew her to bring water
a sudden leap to silt

they built in the adjacent field

map 23

birds lifted suddenly
by their wings
as if in flight
might retake

gravel. purple edges
lace white thorns
what is propelled across water

strike
as in
(she held herself still with a stick

as if to say)
there were hundreds of brown dresses floating among crows
and before that
numerous tiny birches,
waving

i have four dollars and a paper spill
i have not yet called out to you

it came across a browner field, solid, like a soldier

story (clay)

brought red cloth down from the mountain

(frayed)   it spread

                              brick   algebra   allege

a line of thin white soldiers

                    him leaning in sawdust. shadows swiftly across, a
                    color green. avenues the time we. from underneath
                    dripped skirt. played with language and made it
                    (they) built rough. like (black deer drop through
                    pastures) lined, a (revue, county fair, added to stock)
                    (flour and simultaneously) georgette

          wanted green and got a town

(laid down and risen again) the bride pedaling her bicycle (avenues. apparition.
ten notions met at the fork in the creek, climb up to touch the bank)

she left her clothes folded neatly on the pier. jumped in and let the current take her, buick parked where they always parked, purse under the seat muscadine vine and the smell of paraffin. she worked hard around her shrubs, scrip and scrap. taught her daughters to sew. we called her gorgeous but of course she didn't like that. vines came crawling back, a letter on her leg. they say the army was more romantic then. pulled into the drive, saw the empty window as he came. her name meaning theatrical, theater, stagelight. never saw him look so mean, something waving on his arm snapdragon throated as if she too. taut. i will chuck you under the chin, i will lay you down to sleep, earlygirl it's morning. she always knew someday she'd hear that song. morning towing heralds in the birds. keep this comb for me, little dragonweed flower. come back and i will meet you. here by the side of the road. dirt dug in holes and the water leaning cornflowers towing the field, fences radiating inertia. i could take you back but the wire would still be torn. lean down here, pull your back in behind you. stuffed into caps and rivulets, a boy could drown and his mother, here. carry me. she told you when you sneeze to say you sneezed. i taught you that. she wears the blue as if she's the only one, creek a ruined eye lined up the whiskey bottles and shot them down. right after. came home from church and shot those bottles down. one right after the other. and her in the kitchen with her elbows cold in flour

story (wed)

wraps her hands in (tourniquet) swam she is breaking she (time).

by the back porch while the wasps crawl. tender wings

last light a missing page

when the (girl) met the (pony) and gave it apples.
right from the palm of her hand. sugar in the creases,
foot swept summer. heat. brim through

paint stuck the porch to the (batting)   (home)

summer   cough   the smell of (lemon) brass

carry, the signs of soldiers

map 10

in the greening and the sound
girls in bright dresses, a wound that
taking us on the stairway
(shallow break on the northern side
(roots and thistles

who left rustling metal in a ditch
cows among ruins
side of a starling

map 55

sat down and fed ourselves dirt. the color blue

tired spines poking through ash

and the creek sucking its banks. a girl a postcard, long white beard, eyes
like matted straw

she held herself wide by her hands

and fell, gently, into the pond

map 45

a thumbprint a bruise, swirled height
as the note
the final shading
    come down

paperwasps crumbling
the bird who as a finer hour
still water.
regret.
a spring marked with an x, portion of a traveled road

tiretrack

drew arrows in the gravel
north. northeast.
to call a day
birdnest. misting through
an elemental
    come home

slope.
90 degrees—the string stretched
    flat. on finer days the woodcutter
    hauled into the woods
stones gather for a chimney, something buried
    near water—

chokecherry sprawled as if in mourning. she left them out on the back porch to cool, called them in the morning. sodagirl, theater flick. i camped on the side of the brook, thought back to a time i hadn't known. he carried it clear through the woods. the radio on as the train came through, i didn't know you had it in you. why he did mention it. i can't be blessed. these are weeds, girl, and the weeds are winning morning glory buttons the fields. by the early light of day, babygirl it's day. i can't be kinder if i try. your sleeves are missing their buttons. tenderheart, while i was tenderfoot. as if startled, as if sprinkled, as if the sea had found us out. come on down for supper. why let us in when we're standing right here. each one cups a drink, silver spilling cuffs

purse tucked under the seat. clothes in a neatened pile and let the current take her.
tangle her hair and her with those two daughters

daffodils, her pockets sewn with coins. land baked. haven't had a drop of rain, a stitch, a celebration ended. she saw him in the mirror. that year thirty-five at least, and what was before they counted. tied up with ribbon, her listless hair. can't you see that girl needs something. his name, carved in trees. elderberry. they told her rebecca don't go and then she did.

map 4

morning glories choke the field
fenceposts, smooth bottled
watching where the little road
the dip and swing of a hill
coming fast, commingling

dream of going down a road—
    dogs, neighbors, a back creek listing
double daffodils once she planted
spots on the broad road
primrose tumbling
    thrift, thrush
a peony box

where the field turned marshy
and we turned back
tick country

story (creek)

anoint   allege

count backward

dirty fingers

flags held and sky (threaten rain, appendages seep)

land held for generations. who buried there three cows and (rocks gathered for chimney) fireplace. crept to the corner of (feet and feet water collect in pools) red crepe in the mud

if you couldn't hold a pin

couldn't feel your feet, standing in the (water) brought light upon himself. last joined from the county, decades later and his name spelled wrong

we were there   jugs and jars

pencil stub

creek washing. a penchant for (tickseed, nickels, burial) clay

he righted himself and tried again, rope slung over the branch, poison ivy held with a stick (missing *e*) basin, a gorge with a rusting frame. bedsprings, steering wheel, a pin (corroded its rust) of metal

cloth rotted through, a hand with a tireswing on

torn at the base, a lamp in name only. we going wet. when you
pulled, you pulled large, and as girlhood you. don't forget to lie.
still, my little one, and its little white umbrella. a cough at the
door, pressed closely to the hand. baskets for putting into, arranged
for taking. this was the moment we had speaking of. her hand a
sprig of holly

had to start on up. cutting wood and whiskey bottles in piles. and she in the kitchen. could hear him. out there shooting

tickseed gorgeous in the morning. a coat of ruby red. rubbed red.
i loved her more when she was young, but i tried oh how i tried
not to show it. her teeth bent on her lower lip. she's got a spell on
you now, you watch yourself now. legs rubbed raw as onions. there
were spells and then there were spells. five o'clock naps, pressed to
a darkened couch

gutterseed and then there were none. i saw you still that day, the
postoffice unlit. storms headed north. i called you clear out of my
mouth. bandit. don't say no, say no. crimp the edges and pinch
it shut. one alone is teeming and powerful. the packet with its
shoulders clipped, a sawn corner.

and let the current take her. tangle her hair, two beautiful daughters and the one
could even sew

map 19

where willow blows smoke
a line of hunting gear: hands held out in front of the face
august met going
the birds, a thistle patch
(we lit ourselves   lanterns

dust on top of dust
honeysuckle, peony
bricks lined darkly

rows

map 68

hands held fervently against the face
that in knotting. in knowing
red sorrows and awake:

we wrapped ourselves in braids
lined the shelves with paper
pulled tickseed through barbed wire

map 5

we wear cinders in block patterns
(dust torn thick as shoals
needing two and taking three
each hand run softly   thistles
splinters bearing down

he was soft along the edges, hazy
breath white, a gift for salamanders
along the edges of the thistle pool

needing to go down

and the lines toward path: taking up the sparrows

map 67

spelt longing, shell looming against
made the spell and sun   look up
culling the vines and wed

thirty years along the wet
skirts pulled partially around

map 66

aribel.
the flight along the sleeve
the line of a honeybee

thread pouring
water held against the throat

fifty yards to the deep creek bed
waving her arms, and time

map 65

pull hair and white wire
(dear girl
shove westward from the shore
returned thirty years
a girl in limed skirt
and creek water

sleeves of honeysuckle vine
crops lush and abandoned

story (girl)

names by heart

                          moved aside to watch them pass, double lines of
'said' and 'didn't.' weight of denim and sleeves.
collapse across the edges, new growth there where
the scissors went

pocket change

she made me (where) and watched me go   rope swing

a pocket for housing (mockingbirds, lines bright against fog)

        clock   choke   diligent

buttoning

                          she knew 'sandal' and 'watchface.' a tiny prickhole
for sound. (the way the focus on) as light let through
(the smaller the crack the) opening fled

map 88

what went west was found
(dear ben
tiny willow devices
the lungs filled with smoke, supposing
outward toward the lip
white thrush planted in rows

galloping on ahead: rural, its turned up collar
she lived where the trailer went
spit toothpaste toward the ground
(lost in drain and water

(her face   loose

and him out cutting wood when they pulled up. always got to get started. left her clothes folded neatly on the pier. pulled on his overalls and headed out to the woods

map 47

mailbox
siphons edge, hinges
batten

new at nine years

honeysuckle scrabbling, the hardluck flint of a driveway
we could see her from the road

and running our hair came loose

there was something wrong with his eyes
the hill starting where they started

they drew each other playing in the dirt
and she carried that boy like he was her own
breaking the crusts with our feet   lines
showing where

map 77

paid herself handsomely from the till
buckets and contours, eyes letting loose

a coke will cost you five
by degrees into glass
there was sound a torn collar
and the screen door mostly gone

she wed without regret
pulled herself back   lined hills

she gathered the husks and threw them on the compost heap. got into the buick and tucked her purse under. headed out toward the lake

map 14

carried stairwise, back pasture
collated. collected, its leaves and thistles

descend through water

met her in her finer dress. braids
left running, spatula

carry us across. carry

map 89

lip of a pool, burn white
and scatter the scratches of chickens
she was born to know
(grabbing them by the head

there where the little ones played

bergamot, the fine handling of it. they wore their ribbons straight down their backs. eager eyed. i kept a glare for christmas. as sons might return, and then they did. packets of baked goods. each crooning on the radio. a little butternut might do you good. a little goody's powder.

trumpet vine, climbs of ash and salt. a little wilder its leaning.
there were four doorsteps we counted, each a packet of lemon.
elderberry, its fine bark chewed. five now. going down the backside
she stopped and cried. stopped and cried some more. it was elegant
the way she knew me. tipped her hand into the stove

she sat down in the dirt to sing. wire under skirts, her name carved into rubber. honeysuckle vines protruding, we can't imagine. clementine. porcupines. their soft and rubbery soles. as dogs mince backwards, lanterns following their tips. we heard them in the night. elastic to gather the thin sleeves of her nightgown, ourselves to follow the thread

map 2

i was sitting still in the road. the northern side
lights and vines spilled widely

i was calling you down, come down
by the wide stretch of the ditch

(i
scraping metal of thrush and vine

its iron springs

sticks bobbing still by the shore

trumpet vine pulled in bells and tongs, a girl with her best suit on. by a lattice, unleaning. she probes first with her thumb, then her tongue, a man startled and wet. we could hear you miles away. the creek runs back there, no one said it didn't. catch here, on the edge. i saw you start up yesterday, then turn back yes oh yes you did. catch me now. these are bells of lint

tucked her purse under the seat and headed in to pay her respects. lakelight gleaming.
draped the cabinets the wood her whiskey hair

story (wood)

belt buckle, a july full of (boots cracked and peeling)
we heard ourselves manage over the radio. slight
jarring of space, the lines of (fruit trees, apple and
bartlett pear, the bees) what you were dead for

long lines (poured)

sunlight through toast

a window the five o'clock nap, clocks muffle in (she
draped the fabric across her breast) letting white. i
knew as soon as (doors made solid, aching wood)
rusty and crow

shadows spinning across grass

vines uncleared (a small white ledge)
spoons line up in velvet

we were (five and singly) voice too loud for the
hallways. faded deed and a tinspotted letter, held
between the cover and (trees colored red and blue)

lines   mulch   sand over faces

little ones (peeling now) brought back.

count with us, spaces and bars

and she had the two daughters and the one could even sew

map 74

thrush
thrift
that chimney remains

(climbing with one hand up the ladder, snakeskin thread, boards

curl into straw

that they came hunting through. lights like faces, dogs mincing backwards

barn doors shutting out night

found pictures on the floor. torn from a page and ink, webbed into corners

through asking: jennie wolfe
jennie wolfe swerves to

and jenkins creek, the upper branch with the footbridge on

nothing but air
and line to climb with

map 37

added line to line, increments of flesh
span of finger to thumb
gear gathered and moved: spill on wet pavement
that a hill
a spire
ate funnel cakes and limes. filled the slotted calf
shoulder high, a stick to smoke with

music come suddenly
and birds

map 27

bones jutting from the shoulders. roots hanging
thread, the vines just overhead: she smoked
near water. preferred coarser weaves, the sun
bore down. make circles
in the dirt. rescued birds. spill flowers
tired
under grates

map 98

kept combing close to home. fog weather, the sky in needles overhead and as she floated, pulled herself down, clothes on the pier and flooding the water, threads of her hair, birds of her hair, drifting, pulling

map 59

where each of these facing the other
where were there
each of these (their music sudden and melted

couldn't tear more
couldn't let
shining
across water

as if it
(read your mind your
necessarily tender
and culpable at the bone

we are their darlings, little darling, where have you fled

(who expands where

left to gallant that boy that boy gallant

i take you and read you and never let you

go)

story (wake)

crease the pillows every afternoon, five o'clock light
(banish) for resting. there on the couch and the radio
(divorced family of five) we ate turnips and didn't
eat (green)

bellbottom   calliope   (water seepage, the grain of tin)

belonging to a grandmother

(material wealth, the thing called 'saliva')

breastbone pressed to stairs, windows wide

honeysuckle ran red through the basket. soaked in tubs of salt. is this what you mean, you said, when you mean christmas. dirt drive buckling in the heat. rotted by the windows while you slept, my tongue dipped in nectar. poor man's flower, don't be rubbing your feet off. alabaster. i tied my tongue backwards. baskets, their flaunted tongues, red and ruby in the heat

primroses entwined, the leg of the fencepost that he carved upon.
running the length of a mile. what you wanted but couldn't get.
down by the back creek, a little leaning. she came quick, she came
not at all. as quick as you picked them, then they died. lay them
down in a yielding ditch, plenty of room for more. i taught you
that. what could be hotter than pining at suppertime, as once who
told you so.

peony that ethel planted. a friend of mine, a girl, an ebony rib. it'll look good once it stalks, these are the days for stalking, tie that tie and let it see. i gathered the stones as i went, one in each pocket, spilling the rest down my shirtfront. a spade for striking the ground, she lost. go get him. a nerve tangled mess, and the way she left that car cocked dead at an angle. her clothes spilled neatly on the pier.

pinemoss, you thinking of going. there where the elderberry plays. engine song, illicit song. gutterswipe. their chimneys were torn and rickety, that's how i knew it was. their eyes watching, song. eggs dropped by spoons into water. the letter *t* a seed on your finger. close your eyes and swim, here where the cold draft stood and caught them as they fell. the sound of chopping wood and thread in their hair. asphalt crumpling bright buckets with temporal rims. they were nothing, frozen, their little arms soiled. dig in and we can start aright. she watching well watching from the corner. the field all on fire. if you lay your little shift down. if you climb up here on top. i met your mother coming in from the store. powder all down the front of her dress

story (blue)

flash of white   bandage

(camera and puff)

a cap with a single star

> who walked through georgia (flew over water) our
> hands splay against wood. lined up cars to see the
> (metal gate, carnations in bells) tongues held quietly
> behind teeth. apple style

first plea of summer   (beneath) water

mist of   clay to bury and

> he had a dream of tobacco fields

seabirds far inland

    rope

> knotted and tied. metal before its (rusty and crow,
> sugar-palmed) his name, *e* and all, melt (schoolgirl
> handwriting) a box of shells high in the closet. would
> we have slept (hair too fine to lay) would we have
> shelled (biscuits and pies, scrap in the fields) trailing
> a stick behind us

squash vines making their own way. did you pull them in yet yes
you know i did. her clothes piled neatly on the pier. and then her
hair, swirling. one will get you five. i needed a drink and she gave
it to me, her hand on the knob at all times. raking those leaves to
pieces. i never saw her look so mean. frost ladling the branches

map 86

that biting her hair

seaside dust, dry shells

mingling

anoint. annoy. pale backs linger till dusk

we ate with paper spoons

drank

still

map 78

joined there at the hip. hinges along the backside
wet. wept. charging indoors, perfunctory values
while she practiced the organ and the bells toned on

blue grief. knotted, hats with the crosses missing
softball team with matching socks
(and beneath the blue, corduroy blue

the road as it was first laid out. asphalt crumpling, sides in heat
beside herself, tracing a finger, a map
tongue and groove

bled green on white. three-branch creek, painted
a hand covering span

white keel

map 6

called out to his hand, hers
clapped quietly across edges
white chalk for marking: there, where the willows go
(potted shard
bunches of lilies by a gate, hindsight—
wild dogs locked in for the night

a shore for calling

this moment of bent sun: see, where the willows go
wire worn thick under hands

map 81

sat down and ate from a hat. biscuit birding, lines of quail

meredith moving through vines. berries split along her ankle

to hold it up to light, movement

bleed into paper

a girl a cherry tree

by nineteen she had come. stroke and stroke, water shifting

dry banks and throat. capsize

turn a full circle under earth

chokecherry

little nests of kleenex set on fire out in the gravel. stamped out in whiskey delight. he wouldn't miss it couldn't know

map 56

bridge down. what will become
water
we tossed our paper into the creek
blackberry vines
watched it float
chimney remains. and the thrift, spilling droves

as if to brighten a little corner: red for slips, green
spill and earth
what moves inside. a foot, a wrinkled hand
held by the ankle
that the stems together

no division this
red knee parting

cross of a christ. on each stone, where we leaned
careful of our feet. tapered bells, long tables
hurry up and catch
wanders a creek

lines gather, and the slope feeds itself. blue on blue
teeth at the peak

number our steps. wipe them with sand
toward tillaway lake, ribbon fields
at each green point the lashing
knots   burst

crest and creepervine
gathering chokecherry
brought by its roots through the woods
white shirts buried in ribbons

she made biscuits
morning coat

pinemoss left for taking. the titmouse and the rabbit, violets pulled by their chins. come down, oh come down. left after right after left. we gather our hems and rush, and rush across the water. iron chairs placed there on the banks, the little ones dipping their hands. oh you should've seen him coming. it was something buckling up, heaving our chests under water. you look through the air and then you look again.

timpany flower, she knew it, preening on the side of the road. can we stop can we go in. i meant the white one, you knew that didn't you. append. my wrist was as thin, as taut as you know. catch it best you can, then chuck it out the window. a branch for fallen snow. carry me here, by the side of the road. the church with its ruby coat on.

had to start on up. ruby red coat and a button gone. out there chopping wood and
whiskey cold as flour

snowberry limping its way to shore. it's not the plant i like it's you. roots as thick as legs. when he walked in after all that time she seemed to fall, seemed to carry herself down to the floor. it was written all over your face. walk backwards and you'll see it blooming. at night it folds in, a little lace laundry left out to dry. pedal your feet backwards. we were skimming air thrift spilling its banks, a chimney where nevermore. each rock pulled from the earth, sucking itself up. they had two rooms and a porch, two rockers and a dog. we knew him as samuel, her as the one called. rebecca. walnut and oak, a moss that worked its way in. garden rot. you can plant each crevice or you can just spill it in, depends. she smoked and he didn't, hatbrim pulled low overhead.

a string to lead from here to there. tie your mouth up in honey. start with your thumb and walk from there. a broomstick pulling handles. i can't go in no i just can't. sweep the linoleum where it lay cracking. creases beside her eyes, lie girl lie. i kept you in my little box. all this time, and warm drawing bones and arrows in the dirt. she fled before she turned. seashells gathered in rows. by 'sleeves' she meant imminent, the arrival of something bitter. catch me in the air. she turned around twice and on the third time she was it. lemon peel rolled beneath the tongue, teabags left for soaking. i am not no i am not. as salt sprinkled on tails birds crumpled on the pier, small piles of purse and wood. headed in to pay her respects, daughters tucked under the seat. and him out there chopping

map 31

she stood on the lip. of a pool and
tree roots hanging dry, the night the mistletoe
waited to dive. sweeping the water
copperheads, cottonmouths, water moccasins
in the morning when air begins
morning glory. pencil stub
to twine her hands. knotted, corrections
blades of grass with the sun shining through
on the smallest sheaf
altitude

steps painted white in the dusk. five splinters for your hand. if i point one way and you point that way too. five o'clock shadows, the cull of dogs. if you lie still in hay, what happens; memory playing its film. i could've undone you and i didn't. leave her be. there was some kind of emblem posted on the fence. repeated on the door don't knock now no just don't

map 18

held the jar as it jutted into
and the tip, pointed where
(he used his thumb to guide the string

foot and foot, building
torn way over time

to cross and cross again

known by what passed beneath. a fever doll, tapered song
engineered into dusk
hold the watery stream, its buck and clanging

map 3

morning glories arrive in fields
by the early light of day, babygirl it's day
the kindnesses of moss
sleeves missing what pieces
tenderheart, i was tenderfoot
as if the sea had found us out
come on down for supper
we stayed standing
each one cupped a drink

by the early light of day, babygirl it's day
hands stretched and unlocking
look east the eastern field
wrapped in sleeves and trinkets
i carried you down, come down
the sea, permissible tones
come on down, earlygirl it's day
we stayed standing
water in cupped hands

a cap, a cavern, something knotted at the head. we gather with spoons and thread, pressed. each a tongue and stamen. a girl in a woolly coat, lambwhite sweater. rolled edges and hems. we started down the mountain path, keeping time with our sticks. gather here our loamy presence. ancestors locked in their boxes, it's about keeping. quiet on the mountain land drawn and drawn again, lines laid down in pencil and ink. sketch yourself there. chalk and string and the bend of everyday. canopy. you were in the corn. a sleeve a branch a creek running backward. no such thing as a lamppost. you get lost, your voice kind of withers. weather the better for looking, lights left on in the fog

timpany blossoms the way the squash flowers. her breath bright
and loopy, water pouring down. we danced all around you. your
eyes closed. what will a dollar still get you, a coke in bottles so
tight. no air. pin a little hope on me, a little greenery. at last she
suffered in spells. a land a leaden soldier, its rusting all pulled out.

text Garamond   *designer* Claudia Smelser   *printer and binder* Friesens Corporation